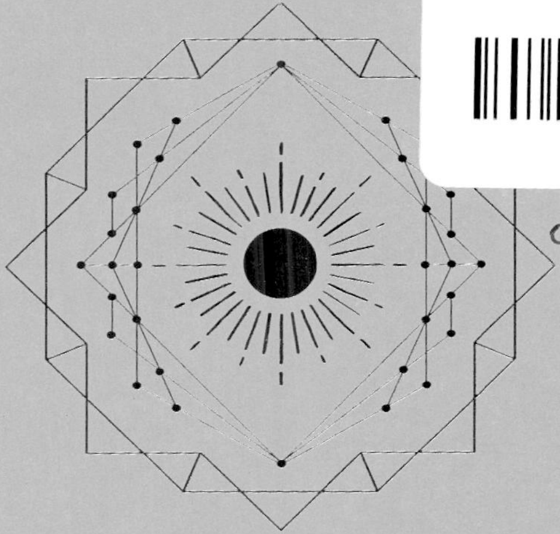

FILLED WITH GRATITUDE

INSIGHTS

an imprint of

INSIGHT EDITIONS

www.insighteditions.com

FILLED WITH GRATITUDE

INSIGHTS

an imprint of

INSIGHT EDITIONS

www.insighteditions.com

FILLED WITH GRATITUDE

INSIGHTS

an imprint of

INSIGHT EDITIONS

www.insighteditions.com

FILLED WITH GRATITUDE

INSIGHTS

an imprint of

INSIGHT EDITIONS

www.insighteditions.com

FILLED WITH GRATITUDE

INSIGHTS

an imprint of

INSIGHT EDITIONS

www.insighteditions.com

FILLED WITH GRATITUDE

INSIGHTS

an imprint of

INSIGHT EDITIONS

www.insighteditions.com

FILLED WITH GRATITUDE

INSIGHTS

an imprint of

INSIGHT EDITIONS

www.insighteditions.com

FILLED WITH GRATITUDE

INSIGHTS

an imprint of

INSIGHT EDITIONS

www.insighteditions.com

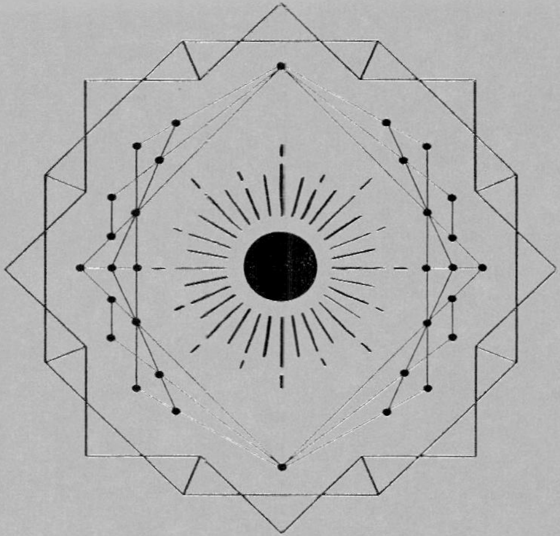

FILLED WITH GRATITUDE

INSIGHTS

an imprint of

INSIGHT EDITIONS

www.insighteditions.com

FILLED WITH GRATITUDE

INSIGHTS

an imprint of

INSIGHT EDITIONS

www.insighteditions.com